First Published In 2019

© Jane Rich

Table of Contents

DAY 1

Almond Cream Cheese Pancakes

Time: 20 minutes

Serve: 4

Ingredients:

- 4 eggs
- 1 tbsp butter, melted
- 1/2 tsp cinnamon
- 1/2 cup cream cheese
- 1/2 cup almond flour

Directions:

- Add all ingredients into the blender and blend until well mix.
- Heat pan over medium heat. Add melted butter in a pan.
- Pour 3 tablespoons of batter per pancake and cook for 2 minutes on each side.
- Serve and enjoy.

Nutritional Value (Amount per Serving):

- Calories 270
- Fat 24.4 g
- Carbohydrates 4.3 g
- Sugar 0.9 g
- Protein 10.8 g
- Cholesterol 203 mg

Creamy Lettuce Salad

Time: 10 minutes

Serve: 2

Ingredients:

- 1 medium tomato, chopped
- 2 cups romaine lettuce, chopped
- For dressing:
- 4 drops liquid stevia
- 2 tsp apple cider vinegar
- 2 tsp lemon juice
- 1/4 cup mayonnaise

Directions:

- In a small bowl, whisk together all dressing ingredients.
- In a large bowl, add chopped romaine lettuce and tomato and toss well.
- Pour dressing over salad and mix well.
- Serve and enjoy.

Nutritional Value (Amount per Serving):

- Calories 135
- Fat 10.1 g
- Carbohydrates 11.2 g
- Sugar 4.2 g
- Protein 1.1 g
- Cholesterol 8 mg

Broccoli Cheddar Soup

Time: 25 minutes

Serve: 8

Ingredients:

- 4 cups broccoli, cut into florets
- 3 cups cheddar cheese, shredded
- 1 cup heavy cream
- 3 1/2 cups vegetable broth
- 2 garlic cloves, minced
- 1 tbsp olive oil

Directions:

- Heat olive oil in a large pot over medium heat.
- Add garlic and sauté for a minute.
- Add broth, broccoli, and heavy cream and bring to boil, reduce heat and simmer for 15 minutes.
- Add shredded cheese and stir continuously until cheese is melted.
- Remove from heat and serve.

Nutritional Value (Amount per Serving):

- Calories 271
- Fat 22.1 g
- Carbohydrates 4.6 g
- Sugar 1.3 g
- Protein 14.3 g
- Cholesterol 65 mg

DAY 2

Healthy Breakfast Muffins

Time: 25 minutes

Serve: 8

Ingredients:

- 4 eggs
- 1 tsp baking powder
- 1 tsp vanilla extract
- 2 tbsp erythritol
- 2 tbsp flaxseed meal
- 2 tbsp heavy whipping cream
- 4 tbsp coconut oil, melted
- 2 servings keto breakfast cereal

Directions:

- Preheat the oven to 350 F/ 176 C.
- Spray muffin tray with cooking spray and set aside.
- In a bowl, mix together coconut oil and keto breakfast cereal until well combined.
- Add remaining ingredients and mix well to combine.
- Pour batter into the prepared muffin tray and bake in preheated oven for 20 minutes.
- Serve and enjoy.

Nutritional Value (Amount per Serving):

- Calories 133
- Fat 12 g
- Carbohydrates 4 g
- Sugar 4 g
- Protein 4.1 g
- Cholesterol 87 mg

Perfect Cheese Broccoli Nuggets

Time: 30 minutes

Serve: 4

Ingredients:

- 1/4 cup almond flour
- 1 cup cheddar cheese, shredded
- 2 egg whites
- 2 cups broccoli florets, cooked until soft
- 1/8 tsp salt

Directions:

- Preheat the oven to 350 F/ 176 C.
- Spray a baking tray with cooking spray and set aside.
- Add cooked broccoli to the bowl and using masher mash broccoli into the small pieces.
- Add remaining ingredients to the bowl and mix well to combine.
- Drop 20 scoops of broccoli mixture onto the prepared baking tray and press into a nugget shape.
- Bake in preheated oven for 20 minutes.
- Serve and enjoy.

Nutritional Value (Amount per Serving):

- Calories 178
- Fat 13 g
- Carbohydrates 5 g
- Sugar 1.3 g
- Protein 11.6 g
- Cholesterol 30 mg

Yummy Caprese Zucchini Zoodles

Time: 25 minutes

Serve: 4

Ingredients:

- 2 tbsp balsamic vinegar
- 1/4 cup fresh basil leaves, chopped
- 5 mozzarella balls, quartered
- 2 cups cherry tomatoes, halved
- 2 tbsp olive oil
- 4 zucchini, spiralized
- Pepper
- Salt

Directions:

- Add zoodles into the mixing bowl and season with pepper and salt. Set aside for 15 minutes.
- Add basil, mozzarella balls, and tomatoes to zoodles and toss well.
- Drizzle with balsamic vinegar.
- Serve and enjoy.

Nutritional Value (Amount per Serving):

- Calories 222
- Fat 15 g
- Carbohydrates 10 g
- Sugar 5.8 g
- Protein 9.5 g
- Cholesterol 13 mg

DAY 3

Protein Breakfast

Time: 10 minutes

Serve: 2

Ingredients:

- 15 drops liquid stevia
- 1 tbsp cocoa powder
- 1 tbsp cocoa nibs
- 1 tbsp chia seeds
- 2 tbsp hemp hearts
- 1/2 oz almonds
- 1 cup coconut milk, unsweetened
- 1 scoop protein powder
- 7 oz firm tofu

Directions:

- Add all ingredients into the blender and blend until you get a thick consistency.
- Serve and enjoy.

Nutritional Value (Amount per Serving):

- Calories 243
- Fat 13 g
- Carbohydrates 11 g
- Sugar 1.4 g
- Protein 21.2 g
- Cholesterol 23 mg

Pumpkin Risotto

Time: 15 minutes

Serve: 1

Ingredients:

- 1 tbsp butter
- 1/2 cup water
- 1 cup cauliflower, grated
- 1/4 cup pumpkin, grated
- 2 garlic cloves, peeled and diced
- Pepper
- Salt

Directions:

- Melt butter in a pan over medium heat.
- Add garlic, cauliflower, and pumpkin into the pan and season with pepper and salt.
- Cook until lightly soften.
- Add water and cook until done.
- Serve and enjoy.

Nutritional Value (Amount per Serving):

- Calories 157
- Fat 11.8 g
- Carbohydrates 12 g
- Sugar 4.5 g
- Protein 3.2 g
- Cholesterol 31 mg

Baked Zoodle

Time: 45 minutes

Serve: 4

Ingredients:

- 2 medium zucchini, spiralized
- 1 cup Fontina cheese, grated
- 2 tsp Worcestershire sauce
- 1/4 cup vegetable broth
- 2 tbsp butter
- 1 tsp fresh thyme, chopped
- 1 small onion, sliced
- Pepper
- Salt

Directions:

- Preheat the oven to 400 F/ 204 C.
- Spray 5*8" baking dish with cooking spray and set aside.
- Melt butter in a pan over medium heat.
- Add onion in a pan and sauté for few minutes.
- Add thyme, Worcestershire sauce, pepper, and salt. Stir for minutes.
- Add broth in the pan and cook onions for 10 minutes.
- In a large bowl, combine together zucchini noodles and onion mixture and pour into the prepared dish.
- Top with grated cheese and bake in preheated oven for 25 minutes.
- Garnish with freshly chopped thyme.
- Serve and enjoy.

Nutritional Value (Amount per Serving):

- Calories 184
- Fat 14.5 g
- Carbohydrates 6.1 g
- Sugar 3.4 g
- Protein 8.7 g
- Cholesterol 47 mg

DAY 4

Delicious Protein Waffle

Time: 20 minutes

Serve: 10

Ingredients:

- 4 eggs
- 4 tbsp coconut oil, melted
- 1 1/2 cups almond milk, unsweetened
- 1 tbsp baking powder
- 1/2 cup egg white
- 1/2 cup coconut flour
- 1/2 tsp sea salt

Directions:

- Preheat the waffle iron to high.
- In a bowl, add all dry ingredients and mix well to combine.
- Slowly add the wet ingredients and mix well and let sit the batter for 5 minutes.
- Spray waffle iron with cooking spray.
- Pour batter into the preheated waffle iron and cook according to the iron instructions.
- Serve and enjoy.

Nutritional Value (Amount per Serving):

- Calories 187
- Fat 16.4 g
- Carbohydrates 6.9 g
- Protein 5.2 g
- Cholesterol 65 mg

Creamy Zucchini Zoodles

Time: 15 minutes

Serve: 1

Ingredients:

- 2 tbsp parmesan cheese, shredded
- 1 zucchini, spiralized
- 1/2 avocado
- 2 tbsp mascarpone

Directions:

- In a bowl, add avocado and mascarpone and mash until smooth.
- Add avocado mixture to the small saucepan and heat until warm.
- Add spiralized zucchini into the saucepan and cook until heated.
- Stir in parmesan cheese and serve.

Nutritional Value (Amount per Serving):

- Calories 327
- Fat 28.8 g
- Carbohydrates 13 g
- Sugar 2.5 g
- Protein 7.2 g
- Cholesterol 25 mg

Creamy Cauliflower Rice

Time: 15 minutes

Serve: 6

Ingredients:

- 1 cauliflower head, cut into florets
- 2 oz cream cheese
- 2.5 oz cheddar cheese, shredded
- 1/4 tsp garlic powder
- 1/4 tsp pepper
- 1/4 tsp salt

Directions:

- Add cauliflower florets into the food processor and process until it looks like rice.
- Transfer cauliflower rice to the baking dish and microwave for 5 minutes.
- Add cream cheese and cheddar cheese and stir until melted.
- Add garlic powder, pepper, and salt and stir well.
- Serve and enjoy.

Nutritional Value (Amount per Serving):

- Calories 138
- Fat 10.9 g
- Carbohydrates 4.3 g
- Sugar 1.8 g
- Protein 6.8 g
- Cholesterol 34 mg

DAY 5

Blueberry Lemon Muffins

Time: 35 minutes

Serve: 12

Ingredients:

- 2 large eggs
- 1/4 tsp lemon zest
- 1/2 tsp lemon extract
- 1/2 cup fresh blueberries
- 1 tsp baking powder
- 5 drops stevia
- 1/4 cup butter, melted
- 1 cup heavy whipping cream
- 2 cups almond flour

Directions:

- Preheat the oven to 350 F/ 176 C.
- Spray muffin tray with cooking spray and set aside.
- Add eggs to the mixing bowl and whisk until well mix.
- Add remaining ingredients to the eggs and mix well to combine.
- Pour batter into the prepared muffin tray and bake in preheated oven for 25 minutes.
- Serve and enjoy.

Nutritional Value (Amount per Serving):

- Calories 191
- Fat 17.7 g
- Carbohydrates 5.4 g
- Sugar 1.4 g
- Protein 5.4 g
- Cholesterol 55 mg

Tasty Zucchini Patties

Time: 15 minutes

Serve: 4

Ingredients:

- 1 large egg, lightly beaten
- 2 tsp coconut oil
- 1/3 cup mozzarella cheese, shredded
- 1/3 cup parmesan cheese, grated
- 1/2 cup carrot, grated
- 1 cup zucchini, grated
- 1/4 tsp pepper
- 1 tsp salt

Directions:

- Add all ingredients except coconut oil into the bowl and mix until well combined.
- Heat coconut oil in a pan over medium-high heat.
- Drop heaping tablespoonfuls of zucchini mixture on a hot pan and cook for 2 minutes on each side or until lightly golden brown.
- Serve hot and enjoy.

Nutritional Value (Amount per Serving):

- Calories 104
- Fat 7 g
- Carbohydrates 2.5 g
- Sugar 1.3 g
- Protein 6.7 g
- Cholesterol 58 mg

Roasted Broccoli

Time: 35 minutes

Serve: 2

Ingredients:

- 1 broccoli stalk, cut into florets
- 1 tbsp butter
- 3 tbsp parmesan cheese, grated
- 3 tbsp extra virgin olive oil
- 1/8 tsp pepper
- 1/8 tsp salt

Directions:

- Preheat the oven to 390 F/ 200 C.
- Add all ingredients into the large bowl and toss well.
- Spread broccoli on baking tray and roast in preheated oven for 25 minutes.
- Serve and enjoy.

Nutritional Value (Amount per Serving):

- Calories 303
- Fat 30.3 g
- Carbohydrates 3.1 g
- Sugar 0.8 g
- Protein 6.3 g
- Cholesterol 27 mg

DAY 6

Healthy Green Omelet

Time: 15 minutes

Serve: 1

Ingredients:

- 2 eggs
- 1 tsp coconut oil
- 1/2 tsp turmeric
- 1/2 avocado, sliced
- 1/2 cup spinach
- Pepper
- Salt

Directions:

- Add eggs, spinach, turmeric, pepper, and salt in the blender and blend until well mix.
- Heat coconut oil in a pan over medium heat.
- Pour egg mixture into a hot pan and cook for 2-3 minutes then flip to other side and cook for 2 minutes more.
- Transfer omelet to a serving plate, add sliced avocado onto half of the omelet, then fold the omelet in half.
- Serve and enjoy.

Nutritional Value (Amount per Serving):

- Calories 378
- Fat 33.1 g
- Carbohydrates 10.6 g
- Protein 13.5 g
- Cholesterol 327 mg

Yummy Baked Broccoli

Time: 20 minutes

Serve: 4

Ingredients:

- 1 broccoli stalk, cut into florets
- 1/4 cup parmesan cheese, grated
- 1/2 cup gruyere, shredded
- 1/2 cup mozzarella cheese, shredded
- 1/2 cup heavy cream
- 2 garlic cloves, minced
- 1 tbsp butter
- Pepper
- Salt

Directions:

- Preheat the oven to 375 F/ 190 C.
- Melt butter in an oven-safe pan over medium-high heat.
- Add broccoli florets in a pan and season with pepper and salt.
- Cook broccoli florets for 5 minutes or until tender.
- Add garlic and stir for 1 minute.
- Add heavy cream on top of broccoli then top with parmesan, gruyere, and mozzarella cheese.
- Place pan in preheated oven and bake broccoli for 10 minutes.
- Serve and enjoy.

Nutritional Value (Amount per Serving):

- Calories 303
- Fat 22.5 g
- Carbohydrates 2.6 g
- Protein 18.3 g
- Cholesterol 75 mg

Yummy Cauliflower Mac n Cheese

Time: 30 minutes

Serve: 4

Ingredients:

- 1 cauliflower head, cut into florets
- 1/4 cup coconut milk
- 1/4 cup heavy cream
- 1 cup cheddar cheese, shredded
- 3 tbsp butter, melted
- Pepper
- Salt

Directions:

- Preheat the oven to 450 F/ 232 C.
- Spray a baking tray with cooking spray and set aside.
- Add cauliflower florets and 2 tbsp butter in a large bowl and mix well. Season with pepper and salt.
- Spread cauliflower florets on a baking tray and roast in preheated oven for 15 minutes.
- Add roasted cauliflower into the large bowl and set aside.
- In a saucepan, add all remaining ingredients and heat over medium heat until cheese is melted.
- Pour saucepan cheese mixture over the cauliflower florets and mix well.
- Serve and enjoy.

Nutritional Value (Amount per Serving):

- Calories 267
- Fat 24.4 g
- Carbohydrates 4.9 g
- Protein 8.9 g
- Cholesterol 63 mg

DAY 7

Baked Coconut Donuts

Time: 30 minutes

Serve: 6

Ingredients:

- 4 eggs
- 1/2 tsp baking soda
- 1/2 tsp baking powder
- 1/2 tsp instant coffee
- 1/3 cup unsweetened almond milk
- 1 tbsp liquid stevia
- 3 tbsp unsweetened cocoa powder
- 1/4 cup coconut oil
- 1/3 cup coconut flour

Directions:

- Preheat the oven to 350 F/ 176 C.
- Spray doughnut pan with cooking spray and set aside.
- Add all ingredients into the large bowl and mix until well combined.
- Pour the doughnut mixture into the prepared doughnut pan and bake in preheated oven for 20 minutes.
- Serve and enjoy.

Nutritional Value (Amount per Serving):

- Calories 132
- Fat 12.7 g
- Carbohydrates 2.5 g
- Protein 4.4 g
- Cholesterol 109 mg

Easy Squash Casserole

Time: 50 minutes

Serve: 4

Ingredients:

- 4 medium squash, cut into slices
- 3/4 stick butter, cut into cubes
- 1 medium onion, sliced
- 1/4 cup parmesan cheese, shredded
- Pepper
- Salt

Directions:

- Layer slices squash, onion, butter, pepper, and salt. Sprinkle with shredded parmesan cheese in a casserole dish.
- Cover dish with foil and bake at 350 F for 45 minutes.
- Serve and enjoy.

Nutritional Value (Amount per Serving):

- Calories 277
- Fat 23 g
- Carbohydrates 9.8 g
- Sugar 4.6 g
- Protein 10.4 g
- Cholesterol 60 mg

Tomato Basil Soup

Time: 45 minutes

Serve: 6

Ingredients:

- 10 tomatoes, diced
- 2 tbsp fresh basil, chopped
- 1/4 cup heavy cream
- 1/4 cup vegetable stock
- 2 garlic cloves, minced
- 1 tbsp olive oil
- 1/4 tsp pepper
- 1/2 tsp salt

Directions:

- Preheat the oven to 400 F/ 204 C.
- Spray a baking tray with cooking spray.
- In a bowl, toss together tomatoes, olive oil, and garlic and spread on a baking tray.
- Roast in preheated oven for 20 minutes.
- Transfer roasted tomato mixture into the blender and blend until smooth.
- Pour tomato puree into a saucepan and heat over medium heat.
- Add stock and simmer for 15 minutes.
- Add basil and cream and stir well.
- Serve and enjoy.

Nutritional Value (Amount per Serving):

- Calories 78
- Fat 4.9 g
- Carbohydrates 8.9 g
- Protein 2 g
- Cholesterol 7 mg

DAY 8

Vegan Hemp Heart Porridge

Time: 10 minutes

Serve: 2

Ingredients:

- 1/4 cup almond flour
- 1/2 tsp cinnamon
- 3/4 tsp vanilla extract
- 5 drops liquid stevia
- 1 tbsp chia seeds
- 2 tbsp ground flax seed
- 1/2 cup hemp hearts
- 1 cup unsweetened almond milk

Directions:

- Add all ingredients to the saucepan and stir until combined.
- Place saucepan over medium heat and cook until just begins to boil.
- Stir once and cook for another 2 minutes.
- Serve and enjoy.

Nutritional Value (Amount per Serving):

- Calories 220
- Fat 16.2 g
- Carbohydrates 11.2 g
- Sugar 2.1 g
- Protein 8.8 g
- Cholesterol 0 mg

Creamy Cucumber Salad

Time: 10 minutes

Serve: 4

Ingredients:

- 1 large cucumber, peeled and cut into slices
- 1 tsp dill
- 2 tsp fresh lemon juice
- 1 small onion, sliced
- 1 medium tomato, sliced
- 1/2 cup sour cream
- 1/4 tsp salt

Directions:

- In a mixing bowl, add sour cream, lemon juice, dill, and salt. Mix well.
- Add tomato, cucumber, and onion into the bowl and stir well to coat.
- Serve and enjoy.

Nutritional Value (Amount per Serving):

- Calories 87
- Fat 6.2 g
- Carbohydrates 7 g
- Sugar 2.9 g
- Protein 1.9 g
- Cholesterol 13 mg

Healthy Roasted Cauliflower and Broccoli

Time: 30 minutes

Serve: 6

Ingredients:

- 4 cups cauliflower florets
- 4 cups broccoli florets
- 2/3 cup parmesan cheese, shredded
- 4 garlic cloves, minced
- 1/3 cup extra-virgin olive oil
- Pepper
- Salt

Directions:

- Preheat the oven to 400 F/ 204 C.
- Spray a baking tray with cooking spray and set aside.
- Add half parmesan cheese, broccoli, cauliflower, garlic, oil, pepper, and salt into the large bowl and toss well.
- Spread broccoli and cauliflower mixture on a baking tray and bake in preheated oven for 20 minutes.
- Just before serving add remaining cheese and toss well.
- Serve and enjoy.

Nutritional Value (Amount per Serving):

- Calories 216
- Fat 5.6 g
- Carbohydrates 8.2 g
- Sugar 2.7 g
- Protein 11.2 g
- Cholesterol 20 mg

DAY 9

Quick Breakfast Cereal

Time: 10 minutes

Serve: 1

Ingredients:

- 1/2 tbsp unsweetened coconut flakes
- 1 tbsp chia seeds
- 1 tbsp ground flax seed
- 2 medium strawberries, chopped
- 1/2 oz pecan halves
- 1/2 tsp vanilla
- 1/2 cup coconut milk

Directions:

- Add all ingredients except coconut milk in serving bowl and mix well.
- Add coconut milk and stir well.
- Serve and enjoy.

Nutritional Value (Amount per Serving):

- Calories 312
- Fat 27 g
- Carbohydrates 14 g
- Sugar 4 g
- Protein 8 g
- Cholesterol 0 mg

Stir Fried Zucchini Tomatoes

Time: 15 minutes

Serve: 4

Ingredients:

- 2 small zucchini, cut into slices
- 1 tsp basil
- 2 medium tomatoes, chopped
- 1 medium onion, chopped
- 1 tsp butter
- 1/4 tsp pepper
- 1/2 tsp salt

Directions:

- Melt butter in a pan over medium heat.
- Add onion and cook until softened.
- Add zucchini and cook for 3 minutes.
- Add tomatoes and basil and cook until zucchini is tender.
- Season with pepper and salt.
- Serve and enjoy.

Nutritional Value (Amount per Serving):

- Calories 43
- Fat 1.2 g
- Carbohydrates 7.7 g
- Sugar 4.1 g
- Protein 1.7 g
- Cholesterol 3 mg

Creamy Mushroom Soup

Time: 35 minutes

Serve: 5

Ingredients:

- 20 oz mushrooms, sliced
- 1 cup coconut milk
- 1 cup heavy cream
- 2 cups vegetable stock
- 4 garlic cloves, minced
- 1/2 onion, diced
- 1 tbsp olive oil
- 1/4 tsp pepper
- 3/4 tsp salt

Directions:

- Heat olive oil in a large pot over medium heat.
- Add mushrooms and onions in the pot and sauté for 10 minutes.
- Add garlic and sauté for a minute.
- Add stock, coconut milk, cream, pepper, and salt. Bring to boil, then reduce heat and simmer for 15 minutes.
- Using blender puree the soup until smooth and creamy.
- Serve and enjoy.

Nutritional Value (Amount per Serving):

- Calories 252
- Fat 23.9 g
- Carbohydrates 9.4 g
- Sugar 4.5 g
- Protein 5.4 g
- Cholesterol 33 mg

DAY 10

Delicious Zucchini Frittata

Time: 30 minutes

Serve: 4

Ingredients:

- 8 eggs
- 1 tbsp basil, chopped
- 1 medium zucchini, sliced
- 1/2 tsp Mediterranean seasoning
- 1 garlic clove, minced
- 2 tbsp olive oil
- 1 cup feta cheese, crumbled
- 1/2 cup olives, pitted and halved
- 1 cup cherry tomatoes, cut in half
- Pepper
- Salt

Directions:

- Heat the oven grill to medium heat.
- Heat olive oil in a pan. Add zucchini and cook until lightly golden.
- Add garlic, Mediterranean spice, and olives and cook for 1 minute more.
- In a bowl, whisk together eggs, pepper, and salt. Stir in feta cheese.
- Add tomatoes to a pan and pour egg mixture. Reduce heat to low and cook for 5-8 minutes.
- Transfer pan to the oven and bake until frittata is set.
- Garnish with chopped basil.
- Cut frittata into wedges and serve.

Nutritional Value (Amount per Serving):

- Calories 321
- Fat 25.7 g
- Carbohydrates 6.9 g
- Sugar 4.3 g
- Protein 17.6 g
- Cholesterol 361 mg

Olive Tomato Cucumber Salad

Time: 10 minutes

Serve: 2

Ingredients:

- 1/4 cup olive oil vinaigrette
- 1/2 small onion, chopped
- 1/4 cup olives, sliced
- 1/2 cup grape tomatoes, cut in half
- 1 large cucumber, chopped
- Pepper
- Salt

Directions:

- Add all ingredients into the mixing bowl and toss well.
- Place salad bowl in refrigerator for hours.
- Serve chilled and enjoy.

Nutritional Value (Amount per Serving):

- Calories 65
- Fat 2.8 g
- Carbohydrates 10.3 g
- Sugar 4.7 g
- Protein 1.7 g
- Cholesterol 0 mg

Green Bean Casserole

Time: 30 minutes

Serve: 4

Ingredients:

- 1 lb green beans, trimmed and cut into pieces
- 2 tbsp lemon zest
- 1/4 cup parmesan cheese, shredded
- 1/4 cup olive oil
- 2 oz pecans, crushed
- 1 small onion, chopped

Directions:

- Preheat the oven to 450 F/ 232 C.
- Add all ingredients into the mixing bowl and toss well.
- Spread green bean mixture into the baking dish and bake in preheated oven for 20 minutes.
- Serve and enjoy.

Nutritional Value (Amount per Serving):

- Calories 371
- Fat 31.9 g
- Carbohydrates 12 g
- Sugar 3 g
- Protein 15.8 g
- Cholesterol 30 mg

DAY 11

Cauliflower Hemp Porridge

Time: 15 minutes

Serve: 2

Ingredients:

- 1 cup unsweetened almond milk
- 4 drops stevia
- 1/2 tsp ground cinnamon
- 1/2 tsp vanilla
- 1 tbsp almond butter
- 1 tbsp chia seeds
- 1/4 cup grated cauliflower
- 1/4 cup hemp seeds
- Pinch of salt

Directions:

- Add hemp, grated cauliflower, and almond milk in a saucepan and bring to boil, simmer for 5 minutes until cauliflower is cooked.
- Add remaining ingredients and stir to mix and thicken.
- Serve and enjoy.

Nutritional Value (Amount per Serving):

- Calories 184
- Fat 14.1 g
- Carbohydrates 7.8 g
- Sugar 0.9 g
- Protein 9.5 g
- Cholesterol 0 mg

Jalapeno Cucumber Salad

Time: 10 minutes

Serve: 4

Ingredients:

- 1 garlic clove, crushed
- 2 jalapeno pepper, seeded and diced
- 1 tbsp seasoning salt
- 1/2 cup sour cream
- 2 tbsp fresh cilantro, chopped
- 2 tbsp fresh lime juice
- 1/2 cup tomatoes, diced
- 1/4 cup onion, chopped
- 4 cups cucumbers, peeled and diced

Directions:

- Add all ingredients into the large bowl and mix well.
- Place salad bowl in refrigerator for 2 hours.
- Serve chilled and enjoy.

Nutritional Value (Amount per Serving):

- Calories 88
- Fat 6.2 g
- Carbohydrates 7.3 g
- Sugar 2.9 g
- Protein 2 g
- Cholesterol 13 mg

Tasty Tomato and Eggs

Time: 15 minutes

Serve: 2

Ingredients:

- 2 large eggs
- 1 tsp olive oil
- 1 tomato, chopped
- 4 scallions, chopped
- 3 egg whites
- Pepper
- Salt

Ingredients:

- Heat olive oil in a pan over medium-low heat.
- Add tomato and scallions to the pan and stir well.
- In a bowl, whisk together eggs, egg whites, pepper, and salt.
- Pour egg mixture into the pan and stir for 3-4 minutes.
- Serve and enjoy.

Nutritional Value (Amount per Serving):

- Calories 133
- Fat 7.5 g
- Carbohydrates 4.2 g
- Sugar 2.3 g
- Protein 12.5 g
- Cholesterol 186 mg

DAY 12

Cauliflower Pancakes

Time: 20 minutes

Serve: 3

Ingredients:

- 2 eggs
- 3 tbsp sour cream
- 3 tbsp butter
- 1/2 tsp pepper
- 1 tbsp flax meal
- 1/2 cup scallions, sliced
- 1/2 cauliflower head, grated
- 1 1/2 tsp salt

Directions:

- Add grated cauliflower and 1 tsp salt in a bowl and mix well. Set aside for 20 minutes.
- After 20 minutes add cauliflower into a muslin cloth and squeeze out all liquid from cauliflower.
- Add squeezed cauliflower into a mixing bowl.
- Add remaining ingredients except for sour cream and butter. Mix well.
- Melt butter in a pan over medium-high heat.
- Once butter melted then add spoonfuls of cauliflower mixture and flatten out into small pancakes.
- Cook pancake for 2-3 minutes on each side or until lightly golden brown.
- Serve with sour cream and enjoy.

Nutritional Value (Amount per Serving):

- Calories 197
- Fat 17.9 g
- Carbohydrates 5.2 g
- Protein 5.9 g
- Cholesterol 145 mg

Roasted Cauliflower

Time: 45 minutes

Serve: 4

Ingredients:

- 1 medium cauliflower head, cut into florets
- 1/2 cup parmesan cheese, shredded
- 3 tbsp extra virgin olive oil
- 2 garlic cloves, chopped
- 1 medium onion, sliced
- 1/2 tsp pepper
- 1/2 tsp salt

Directions:

- Preheat the oven to 425 F/ 218 C.
- Add all ingredients except parmesan cheese into the mixing bowl and toss well.
- Spread cauliflower mixture on baking tray and roast in preheated oven for 35 minutes.
- Remove baking tray from oven. Sprinkle grated parmesan cheese over cauliflower florets and toss well to combine.
- Roast cauliflower again for 10 minutes.
- Serve and enjoy.

Nutritional Value (Amount per Serving):

- Calories 90
- Fat 4.5 g
- Carbohydrates 10.9 g
- Sugar 4.6 g
- Protein 4.3 g
- Cholesterol 3 mg

Creamy Asparagus Soup

Time: 25 minutes

Serve: 6

Ingredients:

- 2 lbs asparagus, cut the ends
- 2 tbsp sour cream
- 6 cups chicken stock
- 1 onion, chopped
- 1 tbsp butter
- Pepper
- Salt

Directions:

- Melt butter in a large pot over medium heat.
- Add onion to the pot and sauté for 2 minutes.
- Add asparagus, stock, pepper, and salt. Bring to boil, cover and simmer for 20 minutes.
- Remove pot from heat and add sour cream. Stir well.
- Using blender puree the soup until smooth and creamy.
- Serve and enjoy.

Nutritional Value (Amount per Serving):

- Calories 73
- Fat 3.5 g
- Carbohydrates 8.5 g
- Sugar 4.3 g
- Protein 4.4 g
- Cholesterol 7 mg

DAY 13

Spicy Egg Scrambled

Time: 20 minutes

Serve: 2

Ingredients:

- 4 large eggs
- 2 tbsp scallions, sliced
- 1/4 tsp black pepper
- 2 tbsp cilantro, chopped
- 1/3 cup heavy cream
- 1 tomato, diced
- 1 Serrano chili pepper, chopped
- 3 tbsp butter
- 1/2 tsp salt

Directions:

- Melt butter in a pan over medium heat.
- Add tomato and chili pepper and sauté for 2 minutes.
- In a bowl, whisk together eggs, cilantro, cream, pepper, and salt.
- Pour egg mixture into the pan and stir until cook and egg scrambled.
- Garnish with scallions and serve.

Nutritional Value (Amount per Serving):

- Calories 376
- Fat 34.7 g
- Carbohydrates 3.7 g
- Sugar 1.8 g
- Protein 13.6 g
- Cholesterol 445 mg

Spicy Lemon Cucumber

Time: 10 minutes

Serve: 2

Ingredients:

- 1 large cucumber, cut into slices
- 1 tsp chili powder
- 1 tbsp olive oil
- 1 tbsp fresh lemon juice
- 1/2 tsp pepper
- 1/2 tsp salt

Directions:

- Add all ingredients to the bowl and toss well.
- Serve and enjoy.

Nutritional Value (Amount per Serving):

- Calories 90
- Fat 7.5 g
- Carbohydrates 6.7 g
- Sugar 2.8 g
- Protein 1.3 g
- Cholesterol 0 mg

Easy Cauliflower Soup

Time: 30 minutes

Serve: 4

Ingredients:

- 1 cauliflower head, chopped
- 4 cups vegetable stock
- 1/2 cup onion, chopped
- 1 tbsp butter
- Pepper
- Salt

Directions:

- Melt butter in a saucepan over medium heat.
- Add onion to the saucepan and sauté for 3 minutes.
- Add remaining ingredients and stir well. Bring to boil, then simmer for 20 minutes.
- Using blender puree the soup until smooth.
- Serve and enjoy.

Nutritional Value (Amount per Serving):

- Calories 50
- Fat 3.5 g
- Carbohydrates 5.4 g
- Sugar 2.7 g
- Protein 1.5 g
- Cholesterol 8 mg

DAY 14

Cherry Tomato Frittata

Time: 20 minutes

Serve: 2

Ingredients:

- 6 eggs
- 1 tbsp fresh basil, chopped
- 1 tbsp fresh chives, chopped
- 1 tbsp butter
- 3.5 oz cherry tomatoes, halved
- 2/3 cup feta cheese, crumbled
- 1 small onion, chopped
- Pepper
- Salt

Directions:

- Preheat the broiler to 400 F/ 200 C.
- Melt butter in a pan over medium-high heat.
- Add onion and sauté until lightly browned.
- In a bowl, whisk together eggs, basil, chives, pepper, and salt.
- Once onion is browned then pour egg mixture into a pan.
- Top with cherry tomatoes and crumbled cheese. Place pan under the broiler and cook for 5-7 minutes.
- Serve immediately and enjoy.

Nutritional Value (Amount per Serving):

- Calories 395
- Fat 29.7 g
- Carbohydrates 8.4 g
- Sugar 5.9 g
- Protein 24.7 g
- Cholesterol 551 mg

Parmesan Garlic Brussels sprouts

Time: 15 minutes

Serve: 3

Ingredients:

- 15 Brussels sprouts, halved
- 1 tsp parmesan cheese, grated
- 2 garlic cloves, minced
- 1 1/2 tbsp olive oil
- 1 1/2 tbsp butter
- 1/4 tsp pepper
- 1/4 tsp salt

Directions:

- Heat olive oil and butter in a pan over medium-high heat.
- Reduce heat to medium and add garlic. Sauté garlic for a minute.
- Add sprouts and cover the pan with a lid and cook for 10 minutes without stirring.
- Top with parmesan cheese and season with pepper and salt.
- Serve and enjoy.

Nutritional Value (Amount per Serving):

- Calories 159
- Fat 13.2 g
- Carbohydrates 9.8 g
- Sugar 2.1 g
- Protein 3.7 g
- Cholesterol 16 mg

Creamy Broccoli Soup

Time: 25 minutes

Serve: 4

Ingredients:

- 5 cups broccoli florets
- 2 garlic cloves, chopped
- 1 carrot, peeled and chopped
- 1 onion, chopped
- 1/2 cup cheddar cheese, shredded
- 2 tbsp sour cream
- 1/2 cup coconut milk
- 15 oz vegetable stock
- Pepper
- Salt

Directions:

- Add stock, garlic, carrots, and onions into the stockpot. Bring to boil, then cover and simmer for 5 minutes.
- Add Coconut milk, broccoli, and pepper and cook for 10 minutes more.
- Add sour cream and stir well.
- Using blender puree the soup until smooth and creamy.
- Top with cheddar cheese and serve.

Nutritional Value (Amount per Serving):

- Calories 148
- Fat 8.8 g
- Carbohydrates 13 g
- Sugar 4.9 g
- Protein 7.6 g
- Cholesterol 17 mg

DAY 15

Almond Blueberry Breakfast Muffins

Time: 25 minutes

Serve: 9

Ingredients:

- 1 egg
- 1/2 cup fresh blueberries
- 1/2 tsp baking soda
- 5 drops liquid stevia
- 1/4 tsp vanilla extract
- 3/4 cup heavy cream
- 1/4 cup butter
- 1/4 tsp baking powder
- 2 1/2 cup almond flour
- 1/2 tsp salt

Directions:

- Preheat the oven to 375 F/ 190 C.
- Spray muffin pan with cooking spray and set aside.
- Mix together almond flour, salt, and baking powder.
- In a large bowl, whisk together egg, butter, vanilla, stevia, baking soda, and heavy cream until smooth.
- Add almond flour mixture into the egg mixture and stir to combine.
- Pour batter into the muffin tray and bake in preheated oven for 15 minutes.
- Serve and enjoy.

Nutritional Value (Amount per Serving):

- Calories 270
- Fat 24.9 g
- Carbohydrates 8.3 g
- Sugar 2 g
- Protein 7.6 g
- Cholesterol 45 mg

Mayonnaise Egg Salad

Time: 10 minutes

Serve: 4

Ingredients:

- 6 hard-boiled eggs, chopped
- 1 tbsp fresh dill, chopped
- 3 tbsp mayonnaise
- 1/2 cup dill pickles, chopped
- 1/4 tsp pepper
- 1/4 tsp salt

Directions:

- Add all ingredients into the mixing bowl and stir well to mix.
- Serve and enjoy.

Nutritional Value (Amount per Serving):

- Calories 142
- Fat 10.3 g
- Carbohydrates 4.1 g
- Sugar 1.4 g
- Protein 8.6 g
- Cholesterol 248 mg

Delicious Cauliflower Chili

Time: 35 minutes

Serve: 4

Ingredients:

- 1/2 cup tomatoes, chopped
- 1 tbsp tomato paste
- 2 garlic cloves, chopped
- 2 cups cauliflower rice
- 1 cup mushrooms, quartered
- 1/2 small onion, chopped
- 1 tbsp olive oil
- 1/4 tsp paprika
- 1 tsp cumin powder
- 2 tsp chili powder
- 1/2 tsp black pepper
- 1/2 tsp salt

Directions:

- Heat olive oil in a saucepan over medium heat.
- Add onion and garlic in a saucepan and sauté for 5 minutes.
- Add cauliflower rice and mushrooms and cook for 10 minutes.
- Add spices and stir for minutes.
- Add tomatoes and tomato paste. Stir well.
- Cover saucepan with lid and cook for 10 minutes.
- Stir well and serve.

Nutritional Value (Amount per Serving):

- Calories 66
- Fat 4.1 g
- Carbohydrates 7.4 g
- Sugar 3.1 g
- Protein 2.4 g
- Cholesterol 0 mg

DAY 16

Broccoli Frittata

Time: 30 minutes

Serve: 4

Ingredients:

- 10 eggs
- 1 avocado, sliced
- 2 oz feta cheese, crumbled
- 1 broccoli stalk, cut into florets
- 1 tomato, diced
- 2 tbsp olive oil
- 1 tsp black pepper
- 1 tsp salt

Directions:

- Preheat the oven to 425 F/ 218 C.
- Heat olive oil in a pan over medium heat.
- In a bowl, whisk together eggs, vegetables, pepper, and salt.
- Add crumbled cheese and stir until combined.
- Pour egg mixture into the pan and cook until sides begin to set.
- Bake frittata in preheated oven until golden brown.
- Garnish with avocado slices and serve.

Nutritional Value (Amount per Serving):

- Calories 369
- Fat 30.9 g
- Carbohydrates 8.2 g
- Protein 17.9 g
- Cholesterol 422 mg

Delicious Fluffy Quiche

Time: 45 minutes

Serve: 6

Ingredients:

- 10 eggs
- 1 cup fresh spinach
- 1/4 cup fresh scallions, minced
- 1 cup cheddar cheese, shredded
- 1 cup heavy cream
- 1 cup coconut milk
- 1 tbsp butter
- 1/4 tsp pepper
- 1/4 tsp salt

Directions:

- Preheat the oven to 350 F/ 176 C.
- Spray 9*13 inch pan with cooking spray and set aside.
- In a bowl, whisk together eggs, cream, coconut milk, pepper, and salt.
- Pour egg mixture into the prepared pan then sprinkle with spinach, scallions, and cheese.
- Bake in preheated oven for 35 minutes.
- Serve warm and enjoy.

Nutritional Value (Amount per Serving):

- Calories 361
- Fat 32.4 g
- Carbohydrates 4.1 g
- Sugar 2.1 g
- Protein 15.5 g
- Cholesterol 325 mg

Spinach Mushroom Soup

Time: 30 minutes

Serve: 2

Ingredients:

- 1 cup baby spinach
- 1 cup cauliflower rice
- 1/4 cup coconut milk
- 1 cup vegetable stock
- 2 tbsp vinegar
- 1/8 tsp nutmeg
- 1 tsp black pepper
- 1 tsp thyme
- 5 garlic cloves, sliced
- 2 cups mushrooms, sliced
- 1 tbsp coconut oil
- 1 tsp salt

Directions:

- Heat coconut oil in a pot over medium heat.
- Add mushrooms, garlic, seasoning, and thyme and sauté for 6-8 minutes.
- Add vinegar and stir well.
- Add coconut milk and stock and bring to simmer.
- Add spinach and cauliflower rice. Stir well and cook for 5 minutes or until tender.
- Serve and enjoy.

Nutritional Value (Amount per Serving):

- Calories 183
- Fat 15.4 g
- Carbohydrates 11 g
- Sugar 4.7 g
- Protein 5 g
- Cholesterol 0 mg

DAY 17

Easy Broccoli Casserole

Time: 30 minutes

Serve: 4

Ingredients:

- 1 cup cheese, grated
- 1/2 cup sour cream
- 1 broccoli stalk, cut into florets
- 1/2 cup cream

Directions:

- Preheat the oven to 350 F/ 180 C.
- Spray oven-safe dish with cooking spray.
- Add broccoli florets to the prepared dish.
- Pour sour cream and cream over broccoli florets. Stir well.
- Top with grated cheese and cook in preheated oven for 20 minutes.
- Serve and enjoy.

Nutritional Value (Amount per Serving):

- Calories 203
- Fat 17.2 g
- Carbohydrates 4 g
- Sugar 1.2 g
- Protein 9 g
- Cholesterol 48 mg

Cauliflower Egg Salad

Time: 20 minutes

Serve: 8

Ingredients:

- 6 hard-boiled eggs, peel and chopped
- 2 tbsp onion, chopped
- 3 tbsp mustard
- 1/3 cup mayonnaise
- 1 head cauliflower, steamed and cut into pieces

Directions:

- Add all ingredients into the mixing bowl and mix well.
- Place bowl in refrigerator for hours.
- Serve chilled and enjoy.

Nutritional Value (Amount per Serving):

- Calories 114
- Fat 7.8 g
- Carbohydrates 6.1 g
- Sugar 2.1 g
- Protein 6 g
- Cholesterol 125 mg

Pesto Spaghetti Squash

Time: 20 minutes

Serve: 4

Ingredients:

- 1/4 cup basil pesto
- 2 cups spaghetti squash, cooked and drained
- 4 oz mozzarella cheese, cubed
- 1/2 cup ricotta cheese
- 1 tbsp olive oil
- Pepper
- Salt

Directions:

- In a bowl, combine together olive oil and squash. Season with pepper and salt.
- Spread squash mixture in a casserole dish.
- Spread mozzarella cheese and ricotta cheese on top.
- Bake at 375 F for 10 minutes.
- Drizzle with basil pesto and serve.

Nutritional Value (Amount per Serving):

- Calories 169
- Fat 11.3 g
- Carbohydrates 6.1 g
- Sugar 0.1 g
- Protein 11.9 g
- Cholesterol 25 mg

DAY 18

Cinnamon Egg Scrambled

Time: 15 minutes

Serve: 2

Ingredients:

- 4 eggs
- 2 tbsp cream
- 1 tbsp butter
- 1/4 tsp ground cinnamon

Directions:

- In a bowl, whisk together cream and eggs until smooth.
- Melt butter in a pan over medium heat.
- Add egg mixture in a pan and cook until the scrambled eggs are cooked.
- Transfer cooked egg scrambled to a serving plate and top with ground cinnamon.
- Serve and enjoy.

Nutritional Value (Amount per Serving):

- Calories 185
- Fat 15.2 g
- Carbohydrates 1.3 g
- Sugar 0.9 g
- Protein 11.2 g
- Cholesterol 345 mg

Roasted Brussels sprouts and Broccoli

Time: 40 minutes

Serve: 6

Ingredients:

- 1 lb broccoli, cut into florets
- 1/2 onion, chopped
- 1 lb Brussels sprouts, cut ends
- 1 tsp paprika
- 1 tsp garlic powder
- 1/2 tsp pepper
- 3 tbsp extra virgin olive oil
- 3/4 tsp salt

Directions:

- Preheat the oven to 400 F/ 204 C.
- Add all ingredients into the mixing bowl and toss well.
- Spread vegetable mixture on a baking tray and roast in preheated oven for 30 minutes.
- Serve and enjoy.

Nutritional Value (Amount per Serving):

- Calories 125
- Fat 7.6 g
- Carbohydrates 13 g
- Sugar 3.5 g
- Protein 5 g
- Cholesterol 0 mg

Creamy Garlic Leeks

Time: 15 minutes

Serve: 4

Ingredients:

- 2 large leeks, sliced
- 2 tbsp cream cheese
- 2 garlic cloves, minced
- 2 tbsp butter

Directions:

- Melt butter in a saucepan over medium heat.
- Add garlic to the saucepan and sauté for a minute.
- Add leeks and cook until softened.
- Remove pan from heat and add cream cheese. Stir well.
- Serve and enjoy.

Nutritional Value (Amount per Serving):

- Calories 105
- Fat 8.4 g
- Carbohydrates 7.2 g
- Sugar 2.3 g
- Protein 1.2 g
- Cholesterol 21 mg

DAY 19

Coconut Chocolate Breakfast Smoothie

Time: 10 minutes

Serve: 1

Ingredients:

- 1 tsp stevia
- 1/2 tbsp cocoa powder
- 1/4 cup cream
- 1/4 cup coconut milk
- 1/2 cup unsweetened almond milk

Directions:

- Add all ingredients to the blender and blend until smooth and creamy.
- Serve immediately and enjoy.

Nutritional Value (Amount per Serving):

- Calories 203
- Fat 19.7 g
- Carbohydrates 7.7 g
- Sugar 3.3 g
- Protein 2.8 g
- Cholesterol 11 mg

Tasty Cauliflower Casserole

Time: 25 minutes

Serve: 6

Ingredients:

- 1 cauliflower head, cut into florets and boil
- 1 tsp garlic powder
- 2 cups cheddar cheese, shredded
- 2 tsp Dijon mustard
- 2 oz cream cheese
- 1 cup heavy cream
- 1/2 tsp pepper
- 1/2 tsp salt

Directions:

- Preheat the oven to 375 F/ 190 C.
- Spray 9*9" baking dish with cooking spray and set aside.
- Add cream in a small saucepan and bring to simmer, stir well.
- Add mustard and cream cheese and stir until thickens.
- Remove from heat and add 1 cup shredded cheese and seasoning and stir well.
- Place boiled cauliflower florets into the prepared baking dish.
- Pour saucepan mixture over cauliflower florets.
- Sprinkle remaining cheese over the cauliflower mixture.
- Bake in preheated oven for 15 minutes or lightly brown.
- Serve and enjoy.

Nutritional Value (Amount per Serving):

- Calories 268
- Fat 23.3 g
- Carbohydrates 4.2 g
- Sugar 1.4 g
- Protein 11.5 g
- Cholesterol 77 mg

Spinach Mushroom Pie

Time: 1 hour 10 minutes

Serve: 6

Ingredients:

- 4 eggs
- 1/2 cup mozzarella cheese, shredded
- 1/4 tsp nutmeg
- 1/2 tsp pepper
- 1/2 cup heavy cream
- 16 oz cottage cheese
- 2 tbsp parmesan cheese, grated
- 10 oz fresh spinach
- 2 tsp olive oil
- 1 tsp garlic, minced
- 8 oz mushrooms, sliced
- 1 tsp salt

Directions:

- Preheat the oven to 350 F/ 176 C.
- Heat oil in a pan over medium heat.
- Add mushrooms and garlic in a pan and sauté until tender.
- Add spinach, nutmeg, pepper, and salt and cook until spinach is wilted.
- Drain spinach and mushrooms mixture.
- Sprinkle parmesan cheese into the 9" pie dish.
- In a bowl, whisk together eggs, cottage cheese, and cream and stir well.
- Add mushroom and spinach mixture and stir well.
- Pour mushroom and spinach mixture into a pie dish and bake in preheated oven for 50 minutes.
- Slice and serve.

Nutritional Value (Amount per Serving):

- Calories 198
- Fat 11.1 g
- Carbohydrates 6.6 g
- Protein 18.6 g
- Cholesterol 133 mg

DAY 20

Easy Chia Breakfast Pudding

Time: 10 minutes

Serve: 1

Ingredients:

- 1/2 cup coconut milk
- 2 tbsp chia seeds
- 2 strawberries, sliced

Directions:

- Add coconut milk and chia seeds into a serving bowl and stir well.
- Top with sliced strawberries.
- Serve immediately and enjoy.

Nutritional Value (Amount per Serving):

- Calories 128
- Fat 11.1 g
- Carbohydrates 9.3 g
- Sugar 1.2 g
- Protein 3.9 g
- Cholesterol 0 mg

Jalapeno Egg Scrambled

Time: 15 minutes

Serve: 1

Ingredients:

- 2 large eggs
- 1 jalapeno pepper, chopped
- 1/4 tsp onion powder
- 1/4 tsp garlic powder
- 1 oz cream cheese
- 1 tsp olive oil
- 1/4 tsp pepper
- 1/4 tsp salt

Directions:

- Heat olive oil in a pan over medium heat.
- Add chopped jalapeno pepper in a pan and sauté until softened.
- Add eggs to the pan and stir until lightly scramble.
- Remove pan from heat. Add cream cheese and spices and stir well.
- Serve and enjoy.

Nutritional Value (Amount per Serving):

- Calories 292
- Fat 24.6 g
- Carbohydrates 3.7 g
- Sugar 1.7 g
- Protein 15.2 g
- Cholesterol 403 mg

Cauliflower Pumpkin Risotto

Time: 20 minutes

Serve: 4

Ingredients:

- 4 cups cauliflower rice
- 1 tbsp olive oil
- 1/2 cup coconut milk
- 1 1/2 cups vegetable broth
- 1 cup pumpkin, grated
- 4 garlic cloves, minced
- Pepper
- Salt

Directions:

- Heat olive oil in a pan over medium heat.
- Add garlic, cauliflower, and pumpkin in a pan and cook until softened.
- Add coconut milk and broth and cook until done.
- Season with pepper and salt.
- Serve and enjoy.

Nutritional Value (Amount per Serving):

- Calories 164
- Fat 11.5 g
- Carbohydrates 13 g
- Sugar 5.7 g
- Protein 5.4 g
- Cholesterol 0 mg

DAY 21

Cheesy Egg Scrambled

Time: 15 minutes

Serve: 2

Ingredients:

- 4 eggs
- 1/4 cup cheese, grated
- 1 tbsp feta brine
- 1 tbsp cream
- 1 tbsp butter
- Pepper
- Salt

Directions:

- In a bowl, whisk together eggs, feta brine, and cream until smooth.
- Melt butter in a pan over medium heat.
- Once butter is melted pour egg mixture into the pan and cook over medium-low heat.
- Once egg scramble is almost cooked, add grated cheese and cook until cheese is melted.
- Serve and enjoy.

Nutritional Value (Amount per Serving):

- Calories 238
- Fat 19.5 g
- Carbohydrates 1.1 g
- Sugar 0.9 g
- Protein 14.7 g
- Cholesterol 359 mg

Delicious Mashed Broccoli

Time: 20 minutes

Serve: 4

Ingredients:

- 12 oz broccoli, cut into florets
- 1/4 tsp onion powder
- 1/4 tsp garlic powder
- 2 tbsp parmesan cheese, grated
- 2 tbsp heavy cream
- 3 tbsp sour cream
- Pepper
- Salt

Directions:

- Steam broccoli florets in a pan for 10 minutes.
- Add sour cream, spices, cream, and parmesan cheese into the bowl.
- Add steamed broccoli florets to the bowl and stir well.
- Mash the broccoli mixture using masher until smooth.
- Serve and enjoy.

Nutritional Value (Amount per Serving):

- Calories 85
- Fat 5.5 g
- Carbohydrates 6.5 g
- Sugar 1.6 g
- Protein 3.6 g
- Cholesterol 16 mg

Creamy Cauliflower and Cabbage

Time: 25 minutes

Serve: 6

Ingredients:

- 2 cups cauliflower florets, quartered
- 2/3 cup coconut milk
- 3 cups green cabbage, chopped
- 1 tbsp olive oil
- Pepper
- Salt

Directions:

- Heat olive oil in a pan over medium heat.
- Add cauliflower and cabbage in a pan and sauté until softened.
- Add coconut milk and stir well. Bring to boil, then reduce heat and simmer for 15 minutes or until sauce thickened.
- Season with pepper and salt.
- Serve and enjoy.

Nutritional Value (Amount per Serving):

- Calories 98
- Fat 8.7 g
- Carbohydrates 5.3 g
- Sugar 2.8 g
- Protein 1.7 g
- Cholesterol 0 mg

DAY 22

Healthy Green Smoothie

Time: 10 minutes

Serve: 1

Ingredients:

- 1/2 scoop protein powder
- 1/4 avocado, chopped
- 1/2 cup cucumber, chopped
- 1/2 tsp liquid stevia
- 1/4 cup cream
- 1/2 cup coconut milk
- 4 ice cubes

Directions:

- Add all ingredients into the blender and blend until smooth.
- Serve and enjoy.

Nutritional Value (Amount per Serving):

- Calories 271
- Fat 20.1 g
- Carbohydrates 11.4 g
- Sugar 2.8 g
- Protein 13.6 g
- Cholesterol 44 mg

Simple Avocado Salsa

Time: 20 minutes

Serve: 8

Ingredients:

- 4 avocados, peeled and diced
- 2 tomatoes, diced
- 1 onion, diced
- 1 chili, chopped
- 1 fresh lemon juice

Directions:

- Add all ingredients into the mixing bowl and mix well.
- Serve and enjoy.

Nutritional Value (Amount per Serving):

- Calories 216
- Fat 19.7 g
- Carbohydrates 11 g
- Sugar 1.9 g
- Protein 2.3 g
- Cholesterol 0 mg

Stir Fried Cabbage

Time: 20 minutes

Serve: 4

Ingredients:

- 1 head cabbage, chopped
- 2 tbsp olive oil
- 1 small onion, chopped
- Pepper
- Salt

Directions:

- Heat olive oil in a pan over medium heat.
- Add onion to the pan and sauté until softened.
- Add cabbage and stir until cooked. Season with pepper and salt.
- Serve and enjoy.

Nutritional Value (Amount per Serving):

- Calories 112
- Fat 7.2 g
- Carbohydrates 12 g
- Sugar 6.5 g
- Protein 2.5 g
- Cholesterol 0 mg

DAY 23

Lemon Strawberry Chia Pudding

Time: 10 minutes

Serve: 4

Ingredients:

- 1 cup fresh strawberries, chopped
- 1 tbsp fresh lemon juice
- 10 drops liquid stevia
- 1/3 cup chia seeds
- 2 cups unsweetened almond milk

Directions:

- In a bowl, stir together almond milk and chia seeds.
- Add in lemon juice and strawberries.
- Mix all ingredients well and place in refrigerator for 4 hours.
- Serve chilled and enjoy.

Nutritional Value (Amount per Serving):

- Calories 112
- Fat 5.9 g
- Carbohydrates 10.5 g
- Sugar 1.8 g
- Protein 4.8 g
- Cholesterol 0 mg

Tasty Greek Avocado Salad

Time: 15 minutes

Serve: 4

Ingredients:

- 1 large cucumber, sliced
- 1 avocado, diced
- 1/2 cup olives, pitted
- 7 oz feta cheese, cubed
- 1/2 onion, sliced
- 1 bell pepper, sliced
- 4 tomatoes, chopped
- For dressing:
- 2 tsp oregano
- 1 tsp garlic, minced
- 2 tbsp red wine vinegar
- 1/4 cup extra-virgin olive oil
- 1/4 tsp salt

Directions:

- In a small bowl, whisk together all dressing ingredients and set aside.
- Add all salad ingredients to the mixing bowl and mix well.
- Pour dressing over salad and toss well.
- Serve and enjoy.

Nutritional Value (Amount per Serving):

- Calories 305
- Fat 27 g
- Carbohydrates 12 g
- Sugar 8 g
- Protein 10 g
- Cholesterol 44 mg

Delicious Cauliflower Chowder

Time: 25 minutes

Serve: 4

Ingredients:

- 1 cauliflower head, chopped
- 1/2 tsp coriander powder
- 1 tsp turmeric
- 1 1/4 tsp ground cumin
- 1 cup coconut milk
- 4 cups vegetable stock
- 2 celery stalk, chopped
- 1 onion, chopped
- 3 garlic cloves, minced
- 2 tbsp olive oil
- Pepper
- Salt

Directions:

- Heat olive oil in a large saucepan over medium-high heat.
- Add celery, onion, and garlic and sauté for 5 minutes.
- Add cauliflower and stir well and cook for 5 minutes.
- Add stock, coconut milk, coriander, turmeric, and cumin and stir well. Bring to boil, then reduce heat and simmer for 15 minutes.
- Season with pepper and salt.
- Serve and enjoy.

Nutritional Value (Amount per Serving):

- Calories 237
- Fat 22.1 g
- Carbohydrates 11 g
- Sugar 5.4 g
- Protein 3.3 g
- Cholesterol 0 mg

DAY 24

Cheddar Cheese Quiche

Time: 50 minutes

Serve: 8

Ingredients:

- 12 eggs
- 3/4 cup butter
- 4 oz cream cheese, softened
- 8 oz cheddar cheese, grated
- Pepper
- Salt

Directions:

- Add half cup cheese to the 10-inch pie pan.
- Add eggs, cream cheese, and butter into the blender and blend until well combined.
- Pour egg mixture over cheese in pie pan. Season with pepper and salt.
- Sprinkle remaining grated cheese over the top and bake at 325 F for 45 minutes.
- Serve and enjoy.

Nutritional Value (Amount per Serving):

- Calories 411
- Fat 38.2 g
- Carbohydrates 1.3 g
- Sugar 0.7 g
- Protein 16.6 g
- Cholesterol 337 mg

Easy Cauliflower Grits

Time: 2 hours 5 minutes

Serve: 8

Ingredients:

- 6 cups cauliflower rice
- 1 cup cream cheese
- 1/2 cup vegetable broth
- 1/2 tsp pepper
- 1 tsp salt

Directions:

- Add all ingredients to the slow cooker and stir well combine.
- Cover slow cooker with lid and cook on low for 2 hours.
- Stir well and serve.

Nutritional Value (Amount per Serving):

- Calories 123
- Fat 10.3 g
- Carbohydrates 4.9 g
- Sugar 1.9 g
- Protein 4 g
- Cholesterol 32 mg

Healthy Spinach Kale Soup

Time: 15 minutes

Serve: 6

Ingredients:

- 1 fresh lime juice
- 1 cup water
- 3 1/3 cup coconut milk
- 2 avocados
- 8 oz spinach
- 8 oz kale
- 3 oz olive oil
- 1/4 tsp pepper
- 1 tsp salt

Directions:

- Heat olive oil in a saucepan over medium heat.
- Add kale and spinach to the saucepan and sauté for 2-3 minutes.
- Remove saucepan from heat. Add coconut milk, spices, avocado, and water. Stir well.
- Using blender puree the soup until smooth and creamy.
- Add fresh lime juice and stir well.
- Serve and enjoy.

Nutritional Value (Amount per Serving):

- Calories 233
- Fat 20 g
- Carbohydrates 12 g
- Sugar 0.5 g
- Protein 4.2 g
- Cholesterol 0 mg

DAY 25

Chia Pumpkin Pudding

Time: 10 minutes

Serve: 4

Ingredients:

- 1/4 cup chia seeds
- 1/8 tsp cloves
- 1/4 tsp nutmeg
- 1/4 tsp allspice
- 1/2 tsp ground cinnamon
- 1 tsp vanilla extract
- 12 drops stevia
- 3/4 cup pumpkin puree
- 1 1/2 cups coconut milk

Directions:

- In a bowl, whisk together coconut milk, vanilla, pumpkin purees, and spices.
- Add chia seeds and stir well.
- Place bowl in refrigerator for overnight.
- Serve chilled and enjoy.

Nutritional Value (Amount per Serving):

- Calories 97
- Fat 7.2 g
- Carbohydrates 8.4 g
- Sugar 1.7 g
- Protein 2.6 g
- Cholesterol 0 mg

Simple Tomato Cucumber Salad

Time: 20 minutes

Serves: 6

Ingredients:

- 3 cups cucumbers, sliced
- 3 tomatoes, sliced
- 1/4 cup basil, chopped
- 1/3 cup onion, chopped
- For dressing:
- 3/4 cup apple cider vinegar
- 1/4 cup olive oil
- 1/2 tsp dill weeds
- 1/2 tbsp red wine vinegar
- 1/4 tsp pepper
- 1/4 tsp salt

Directions:

- In a small bowl, mix together all dressing ingredients.
- In a large bowl, add all salad ingredients and mix well.
- Pour dressing over salad and toss well.
- Serve and enjoy.

Nutritional Value (Amount per Serving):

- Calories 101
- Fat 8.6 g
- Carbohydrates 5.3 g
- Sugar 2.9 g
- Protein 1 g
- Cholesterol 0 mg

Perfect Cheese Mushroom Frittata

Time: 30 minutes

Serve: 2

Ingredients:

- 6 eggs
- 5 oz mushrooms, sliced
- 4 oz goat cheese, crumbled
- 2 oz butter
- 2 oz scallions, chopped
- 3 oz fresh spinach
- Pepper
- Salt

Directions:

- Preheat the oven to 350 F/ 176 C.
- Whisk eggs, cheese, pepper, and salt in a bowl.
- Melt butter in a pan over medium heat.
- Add mushrooms and scallions to the pan and sauté for 5-10 minutes.
- Add spinach and sauté for 2 minutes.
- Pour egg mixture into the pan. Place pan in preheated oven and bake for 20 minutes.
- Serve and enjoy.

Nutritional Value (Amount per Serving):

- Calories 682
- Fat 56.7 g
- Carbohydrates 8.3 g
- Sugar 4.3 g
- Protein 38.1 g
- Cholesterol 612 mg

DAY 26

Moist Cheddar Broccoli Muffins

Time: 40 minutes

Serve: 6

Ingredients:

- 4 eggs
- 1/3 cup unsweetened almond milk
- 1/4 tsp sage powder
- 1/2 tsp garlic powder
- 1/2 tsp black pepper
- 1 tsp parsley
- 2 tsp oregano
- 1/4 tsp baking soda
- 1/2 tsp baking powder
- 1 3/4 cup almond flour
- 3.5 oz broccoli, slice
- 4.5 oz cheddar cheese, grated
- 2 tbsp butter, melted
- 1 tbsp apple cider vinegar
- 1/2 tsp salt

Directions:

- Preheat the oven to 400 F/ 200 C.
- Spray muffin tray with cooking spray and set aside.
- In a large bowl, mix together vinegar and almond milk and let sit for 5 minutes.
- Add butter and eggs and mix well.
- In another bowl, mix together all dry ingredients.
- Add wet ingredients to the dry ingredients and mix well.

- Add cheddar cheese and broccoli and mix again.
- Pour batter into the prepared muffin tray and bake in preheated oven for 30 minutes.
- Serve and enjoy.

Nutritional Value (Amount per Serving):

- Calories 360
- Fat 30.5 g
- Carbohydrates 9.6 g
- Sugar 1.9 g
- Protein 16.7 g
- Cholesterol 142 mg

Garlic Eggplant Salad

Time: 45 minutes

Serves: 6

Ingredients:

- 1 lb eggplant, cut into slices
- 1/2 tsp paprika
- 1 tsp ground cumin
- 1 garlic cloves, grated
- 1/4 cup extra-virgin olive oil
- 1 tbsp fresh lemon juice
- 1 tbsp parsley, chopped
- 1 tbsp cilantro, chopped
- 1/2 tsp salt

Directions:

- Preheat the oven to 400 F/ 204 C.
- Coat eggplant slices with 2 tbsp oil.
- Place eggplant slices onto a baking tray and bake in preheated oven for 25 minutes.
- In a bowl, mix together all remaining ingredients and pour over eggplant slices.
- Mix well and serve.

Nutritional Value (Amount per Serving):

- Calories 94
- Fat 8.7 g
- Carbohydrates 5 g
- Sugar 2.4 g
- Protein 0.9 g
- Cholesterol 0 mg

Cauliflower Rice Pilaf

Time: 20 minutes

Serve: 6

Ingredients:

- 6 cups cauliflower rice
- 3/4 cup vegetable stock
- 1 1/2 cups onion, diced
- 3 garlic cloves, minced
- 2 tbsp olive oil
- 1/4 cup butter
- Pepper
- Salt

Directions:

- Heat olive oil and butter in a large pan over medium heat.
- Add onion and garlic and sauté until translucent. Season with pepper and salt.
- Add cauliflower rice and stock to the pan and mix well to combine.
- Cook cauliflower rice until all liquid has absorbed.
- Season with pepper and salt.
- Serve and enjoy.

Nutritional Value (Amount per Serving):

- Calories 148
- Fat 12 g
- Carbohydrates 8.8 g
- Sugar 3.9 g
- Protein 2.5 g
- Cholesterol 20 mg

DAY 27

Delicious Cauliflower Fried Rice

Time: 15 minutes

Serve: 6

Ingredients:

- 3 cups cauliflower rice
- 1 tbsp coconut aminos
- 2 tbsp unsweetened almond milk
- 3 eggs, lightly beaten
- 3 garlic cloves, minced
- 3 tbsp olive oil
- 1 small onion, chopped

Directions:

- Heat olive oil in a pan over medium-high heat.
- Add onion and garlic and sauté until softened.
- Add cauliflower and stir well and push to the side.
- Mix together almond milk and eggs and pour into the pan and cook scrambled.
- Stir scrambled eggs into the cauliflower rice.
- Add coconut aminos and stir well and cook for 2 minutes more.
- Serve and enjoy.

Nutritional Value (Amount per Serving):

- Calories 114
- Fat 9.3 g
- Carbohydrates 5 g
- Protein 4 g
- Cholesterol 82 mg

Eggplant Spinach Salad

Time: 30 minutes

Serves: 4

Ingredients:

- 1 tbsp onion, chopped
- 1 tbsp oregano, chopped
- 5 oz fresh spinach
- 1 tbsp sun-dried tomatoes, chopped
- 1 tbsp parsley, chopped
- 1 tbsp mint, chopped
- 1 large eggplant, cut into slices
- For dressing:
- 1 tsp Dijon mustard
- 1 tsp tahini
- 2 garlic cloves, minced
- 1/4 cup olive oil
- 1/2 fresh lemon juice
- 1/2 tsp paprika

Directions:

- Place sliced eggplants into the bowl and season with salt. Set aside for minutes.
- In a small bowl, mix together all dressing ingredients. Set aside.
- Heat grill to medium-high heat.
- In a large bowl, add onion, sun-dried tomatoes, spinach, and herbs.
- Rinse eggplant slices and pat dry with paper towel.
- Brush eggplant slices with oil and grill on medium high heat for 3 minutes on each side.
- Cut grilled eggplant slices into quarters.
- Add eggplant to the large bowl and pour dressing over salad.
- Toss well and serve.

Nutritional Value (Amount per Serving):

- Calories 162
- Fat 13.9 g
- Carbohydrates 10.2 g
- Sugar 3.9 g
- Protein 2.8 g
- Cholesterol 0 mg

Hearty Broccoli Cauliflower Soup

Time: 7 hours 30 minutes

Serve: 16

Ingredients:

- 2 cups parmesan cheese, grated
- 4 cups cheddar cheese, shredded
- 2 cups heavy cream
- 4 cups vegetable stock
- 1 1/2 lbs broccoli, cut into florets
- 1 medium cauliflower head, cut into florets
- 4 garlic cloves, minced
- 1 medium onion, chopped
- 2 tbsp butter
- Pepper
- Salt

Directions:

- Melt butter in a pan over medium heat.
- Add garlic and onion and sauté until caramelized, about 20 minutes.
- Add garlic-onion mixture to the slow cooker.
- Add broccoli, heavy cream, cauliflower, pepper, and salt into the slow cooker and mix well.
- Cover slow cooker with lid and cook on high for 6 hours.
- Using blender puree the soup until smooth and creamy.
- Add parmesan cheese and cheddar cheese. Stir well and cook for 1 hour more.
- Serve and enjoy.

Nutritional Value (Amount per Serving):

- Calories 281
- Fat 21.2 g
- Carbohydrates 6.5 g
- Protein 15.4 g
- Cholesterol 69 mg

DAY 28

Breakfast Granola

Time: 15 minutes

Serve: 5

Ingredients:

- 2 tbsp coconut oil, melted
- 4 packets Splenda
- 2 tsp cinnamon
- 1 cup walnuts, diced
- 1 cup unsweetened coconut flakes
- 1 cup sliced almonds

Directions:

- Preheat the oven to 375 F/ 190 C.
- Spray a baking tray with cooking spray and set aside.
- Add all ingredients into the medium bowl and toss well.
- Spread bowl mixture on a prepared baking tray and bake in preheated oven for 10 minutes.
- Serve with almond milk and enjoy.

Nutritional Value (Amount per Serving):

- Calories 458
- Fat 42.5 g
- Carbohydrates 13.7 g
- Sugar 2.7 g
- Protein 11.7 g
- Cholesterol 0 mg

Healthy Carrot Cabbage Salad

Time: 50 minutes

Serve: 4

Ingredients:

- 3 cups cabbage, shredded
- 1 carrot, shredded
- 1 turnip, shredded
- 1/4 tsp dill
- 1 green pepper, chopped
- 1 tsp salt

Directions:

- Add cabbage and salt in a bowl. Cover bowl and set aside for 40 minutes.
- Wash and cabbage and dry well.
- Add cabbage in a bowl with remaining ingredients and toss well.
- Serve and enjoy.

Nutritional Value (Amount per Serving):

- Calories 34
- Fat 0.1 g
- Carbohydrates 7.9 g
- Sugar 4.3 g
- Protein 1.3 g
- Cholesterol 0 mg

Creamy Cauliflower Mash

Time: 25 minutes

Serve: 6

Ingredients:

- 1 large cauliflower head, cut into florets
- 2 garlic cloves, minced
- 1/2 cup sour cream
- 3 tbsp creamy horseradish
- 3 tbsp butter
- 1/2 parmesan cheese, grated
- 2 green onions, chopped
- Pepper
- Salt

Directions:

- Add cauliflower florets to the pot then pour water to cover cauliflower florets.
- Cover pot and cook cauliflower for 15 minutes. Drain water well and transfer cauliflower to the bowl.
- Add remaining ingredients to the cauliflower bowl and mash until smooth and creamy.
- Serve and enjoy.

Nutritional Value (Amount per Serving):

- Calories 253
- Fat 17.4 g
- Carbohydrates 10.5 g
- Sugar 3.5 g
- Protein 11.6 g
- Cholesterol 44 mg

DAY 29

Crustless Vegetable Quiche

Time: 50 minutes

Serve: 6

Ingredients:

- 8 egg whites
- 4 pieces roasted red peppers, sliced
- 1/2 cup cherry tomatoes, halved
- 1 cup gruyere cheese, shredded
- 1/4 cup onion, diced
- 2 cups steamed spinach, squeeze out excess liquid
- 1 garlic cloves, minced
- 1/2 cup coconut milk
- Pepper
- Salt

Directions:

- Preheat the oven to 350 F/ 176 C.
- Spray pan with cooking spray and heat over medium-high heat.
- Add garlic and onion and sauté for minutes or until softened.
- In a bowl, whisk together egg whites, cheese, and coconut milk.
- Add sautéed onion and garlic into the egg mixture and stir well.
- Layer tomatoes, roasted peppers, and spinach in a pie dish. Pour egg mixture over the vegetables.
- Bake in preheated oven for 40 minutes.
- Serve and enjoy.

Nutritional Value (Amount per Serving):

- Calories 154
- Fat 10.8 g
- Carbohydrates 3.8 g
- Sugar 2.2 g
- Protein 11.2 g
- Cholesterol 20 mg

Delicious Eggplant Zucchini Casserole

Time: 50 minutes

Serve: 6

Ingredients:

- 3 zucchini, sliced
- 4 tbsp basil, chopped
- 3 oz parmesan cheese, grated
- 1/4 cup parsley, chopped
- 1 cup cherry tomatoes, halved
- 1 medium eggplant, sliced
- 1 tbsp olive oil
- 3 garlic cloves, minced
- 1/4 tsp pepper
- 1/4 tsp salt

Directions:

- Preheat the oven to 350 F/ 176 C.
- Spray baking dish with cooking spray and set aside.
- Add all ingredients into the large bowl and toss well to combine.
- Pour eggplant mixture into prepared dish and bake in preheated oven for 35 minutes.
- Serve and enjoy.

Nutritional Value (Amount per Serving):

- Calories 109
- Fat 5.8 g
- Carbohydrates 10 g
- Sugar 4.8 g
- Protein 7 g
- Cholesterol 10 mg

Sauteed Onion Brussels sprouts

Time: 25 minutes

Serve: 6

Ingredients:

- 2 lbs Brussels sprouts, remove stems and shred Brussels sprouts
- 3 garlic cloves, minced
- 1 1/2 tbsp olive oil
- 2 oz onion, minced
- Pepper
- Salt

Directions:

- Heat olive oil in a large pan over medium heat.
- Add garlic and onion and sauté for 5 minutes.
- Add Brussels sprouts and sauté over medium-high heat for 5-7 minutes or until tender and crisp.
- Season with pepper and salt.
- Serve and enjoy.

Nutritional Value (Amount per Serving):

- Calories 76
- Fat 3 g
- Carbohydrates 11 g
- Sugar 2.8 g
- Protein 4 g
- Cholesterol 0 mg

DAY 30

Quick Pumpkin Muffins

Time: 10 minutes

Serve: 2

Ingredients:

- 1 egg
- 1 1/2 tsp pumpkin spice
- 1/4 tsp baking powder
- 2 tbsp pumpkin puree
- 2 tbsp swerve
- 2 tbsp ground flaxseed
- 2 tbsp almond flour

Directions:

- Spray two ramekins with cooking spray.
- In a bowl, mix together pumpkin puree and egg.
- In another bowl, mix together almond flour, pumpkin spice, baking powder, swerve, and ground flaxseed.
- Pour pumpkin and egg mixture into the almond flour mixture and mix well.
- Pour mixture into the prepared ramekins and microwave for 1-2 minutes.
- Serve and enjoy.

Nutritional Value (Amount per Serving):

- Calories 132
- Fat 9.4 g
- Carbohydrates 8.1 g
- Protein 6 g
- Cholesterol 82 mg

Avocado Kale Salad

Time: 15 minutes

Serve: 4

Ingredients:

- 1/2 lb kale, chopped
- 1/4 cup parsley, chopped
- 1 avocado, peeled and sliced
- 2 tbsp mayonnaise
- 1 tbsp ginger, grated
- 2 fresh scallions, chopped

Directions:

- Add all ingredients into the mixing bowl and toss well.
- Serve and enjoy.

Nutritional Value (Amount per Serving):

- Calories 168
- Fat 12.4 g
- Carbohydrates 13 g
- Sugar 1 g
- Protein 3.1 g
- Cholesterol 2 mg

Zucchini in Creamy Pesto

Time: 25 minutes

Serve: 3

Ingredients:

- 3 medium zucchini, cut zucchini into ribbons
- 1/2 tsp salt
- 1 tbsp olive oil
- For pesto:
- 1/4 cup water
- 1/4 cup parmesan cheese, grated
- 1 tbsp fresh lemon juice
- 2 garlic cloves
- 1/4 cup walnuts
- 1 cup fresh basil
- 1/2 avocado, diced

Directions:

- Add zucchini ribbons and salt into the colander and toss well. Set aside.
- Add all pesto ingredients into the blender and blend until smooth and creamy.
- Heat olive oil in a pan over medium heat.
- Add zucchini ribbons in the pan and sauté for 4-5 minutes or until softened.
- Remove pan from heat and add pesto to the zucchini ribbons and toss gently.
- Serve and enjoy.

Nutritional Value (Amount per Serving):

- Calories 211
- Fat 16.2 g
- Carbohydrates 10.8 g
- Sugar 3.8 g
- Protein 7.8 g
- Cholesterol 10 mg

Printed in Great Britain
by Amazon